Let's Play Dress Up

I WANT TO BE A ROBOT

Rebekah Joy Shirley
Photography by Chris Fairclough

WINDMILL
BOOKS

New York

Published in 2012 by Windmill Books, An Imprint of Rosen Publishing
29 East 21st Street, New York, NY 10010

Series concept: Discovery Books Ltd, 2 College Street, Ludlow, Shropshire SY8 1AN, UK
www.discoverybooks.net

Managing editor: Laura Durman
Editor: Rebecca Hunter
Designer: Blink Media
Photography: Chris Fairclough

Library of Congress Cataloging-in-Publication Data

Shirley, Rebekah Joy.
 I want to be a robot / by Rebekah Joy Shirley. — 1st ed.
   p. cm. — (Let's play dress up)
 Includes bibliographical references and index.
 Includes index.
 ISBN 978-1-61533-357-8 (library binding) — ISBN 978-1-61533-395-0 (pbk.) — ISBN 978-1-61533-460-5 (6-pack)
 1. Handicraft—Juvenile literature. 2. Children's costumes—Juvenile literature. 3. Androids—Juvenile literature. I. Title.
 TT160.S395 2012
 646.4'78—dc22
                              2010050404

The author and photographer would like to acknowledge the following for their help in preparing this book:
the staff and pupils of Chad Vale Primary School, Malachi Clearkin, Suchir Gella, Rosie Palmer-Downes.

Printed in China

CPSIA Compliance Information: Batch #AS2011WM: For Further Information contact Windmill Books, New York, New York at 1-866-478-0556

SL001745US

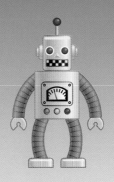

CONTENTS

Some of the projects in this book may require the use of a craft knife. We would advise that young children are supervised by a responsible adult.

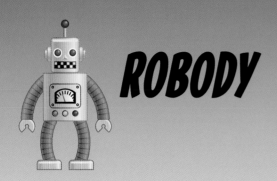

ROBODY

Robots are very powerful machines. Their power source is stored in their upper bodies.

Make your own protective casing using:

A large cardboard box (that will fit over your chest)
A pair of scissors
Colored paints and a paintbrush
A ruler
A black marker pen
Cardboard
Gold elastic

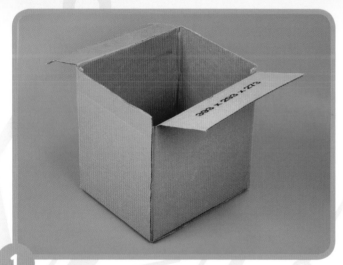

1 Open up the top of the cardboard box and cut the flaps off two opposite sides.

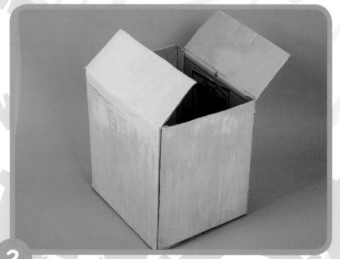

2 Open up the bottom of the box and paint the whole box in one color.

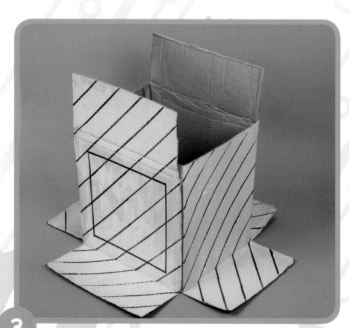

3 Using a ruler and a marker pen draw diagonal lines across the box. Draw a large square on the front.

4 Paint in between the lines to make the box striped. Paint the square too.

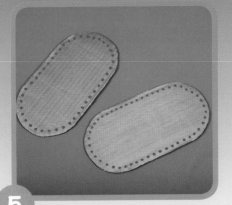

5 Cut two oval shapes out of cardboard, approximately 5 in. long and 2 ½ in. wide. Paint them and add some dots around the edges. These will be the robot's shoulders.

6 Ask an adult to help you make two small holes 1 ½ in. apart on each end of the strips.

7 Make two holes in each corner of the two flaps at the top of the box.

8 Use gold elastic to **attach** the shoulders to the flaps.

Now that you've made your robot body, get ready to decorate it!

GADGETS AND GIZMOS

A robot has many different displays and dials on its body. Make a set using shiny and brightly colored things.

1 Cut a semicircle out of colored cardboard. Decorate it with strips of gold paper.

2 Draw a circle on the back of another piece of colored cardboard. Then draw shapes around the edge of the circle to make a cog-wheel shape.

3 Cut the cog out and decorate the colored side with sequins.

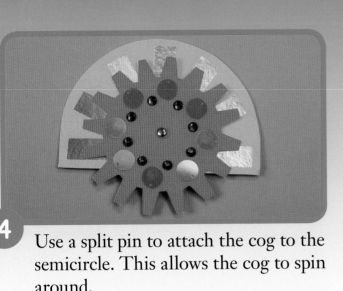

With your control panels and gadgets working you can get ready for some robo-action!

4 Use a split pin to attach the cog to the semicircle. This allows the cog to spin around.

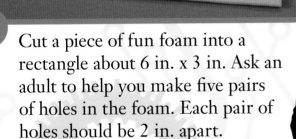

5 Cut a piece of fun foam into a rectangle about 6 in. x 3 in. Ask an adult to help you make five pairs of holes in the foam. Each pair of holes should be 2 in. apart.

TIP:
Attach your gadgets to your robot's body with Velcro. Think up some other gadgets you could make and attach.

6 Thread buttons onto pieces of wool. Thread the wool through the holes in the foam and tie a knot at the back. The buttons will slide up and down the wool.

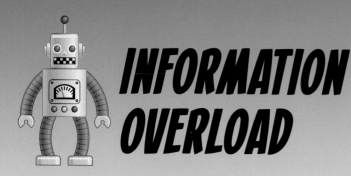

INFORMATION OVERLOAD

A robot's body has many tubes to carry wires from one part of its body to another. Lots of information is passed along these wires.

1 Cut the foam pipe in half.

TIP:
The holes should be slightly smaller than the end of the foam pipe. If the holes are too big, the pipe will not stay in place.

2 Ask an adult to cut two holes in each side of your robot's body.

3 Push the foam pipe through the holes.

4 Use a pen to make six holes in the box between the foam pipes.

5 Thread plastic craft string through the holes and tie together inside.

Now you are ready to do some serious calculations!

LIGHT ME UP

Robots often have flashing lights. They use the lights to flash warnings and coded messages to each other.

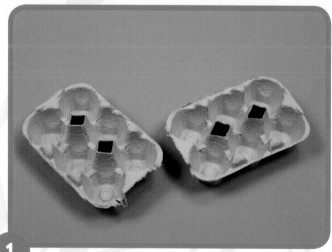

1 Cut off the points inside the the egg box halves.

2 Glue the edges of the holes together to close the gaps. Hold in place with clothespins until the glue dries.

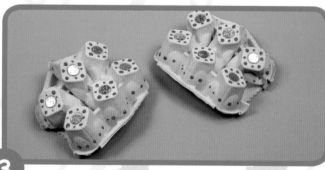

3 Paint the egg boxes. Decorate them with sequins and a different colored paint.

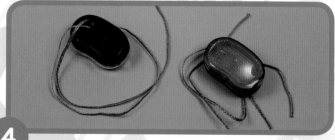

4 Tie gold elastic around the clips at the back of the bicycle lights.

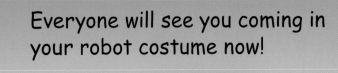

Everyone will see you coming in your robot costume now!

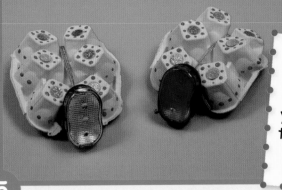

TIP: Make sure that you can still reach the button to turn the lights on!

5 Attach the lights to the egg boxes by tying the gold elastic down their centers.

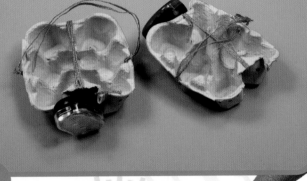

6 Ask an adult to help you make holes in the middle of each side of the egg boxes.

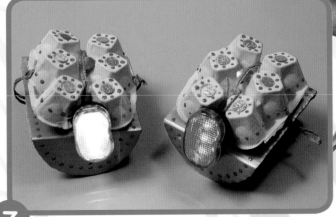

7 Thread some more gold elastic through the holes and tie around the robot's shoulders.

11

BRAIN POWER

A robot's head is where it receives its messages. It needs a strong **antenna** to carry information to its computer "brain."

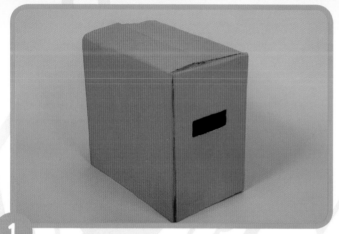

1 Ask an adult to help you cut out a rectangular hole in the box to make an eye-hole (about 6 in. x 3 in.). Then paint the box.

2 When the paint is dry, decorate your robot's face with sequins, paint, and colored paper.

3 Paint two egg box lids and two bottle lids. Use colored paper, paint, and sequins to decorate them.

Now you can look and think like a robot!

4 Ask an adult to cut the top off an empty plastic bottle. Then cover it with newspaper strips and glue.

5 Paint the bottle top and glue it to the top of the box. Glue the bottle lids to the egg box lids and glue onto each side of the box.

6 Thread the pipe cleaners into the straws. Bend the pipe cleaners to make an antenna shape. Insert the antenna into the plastic bottle top and glue in place.

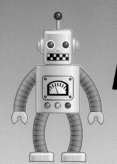

ROBO-LEGS

A robot's body and head can be very heavy, so robots need to have strong, sturdy legs.

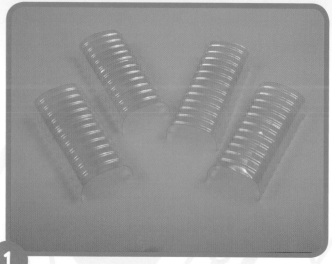

1 Ask an adult to cut the top and bottom off the empty plastic bottles. Then cut the bottles in half **lengthwise.**

TIP: The loop of elastic should fit snugly around your leg.

2 Cover all of the edges with masking tape then paint the half-bottles.

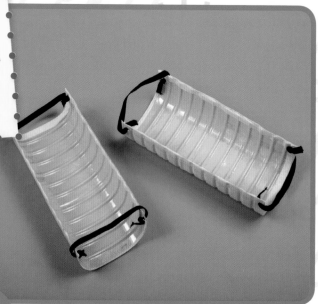

3 Punch holes in each corner of the half-bottles. Thread elastic through the holes and knot each end.

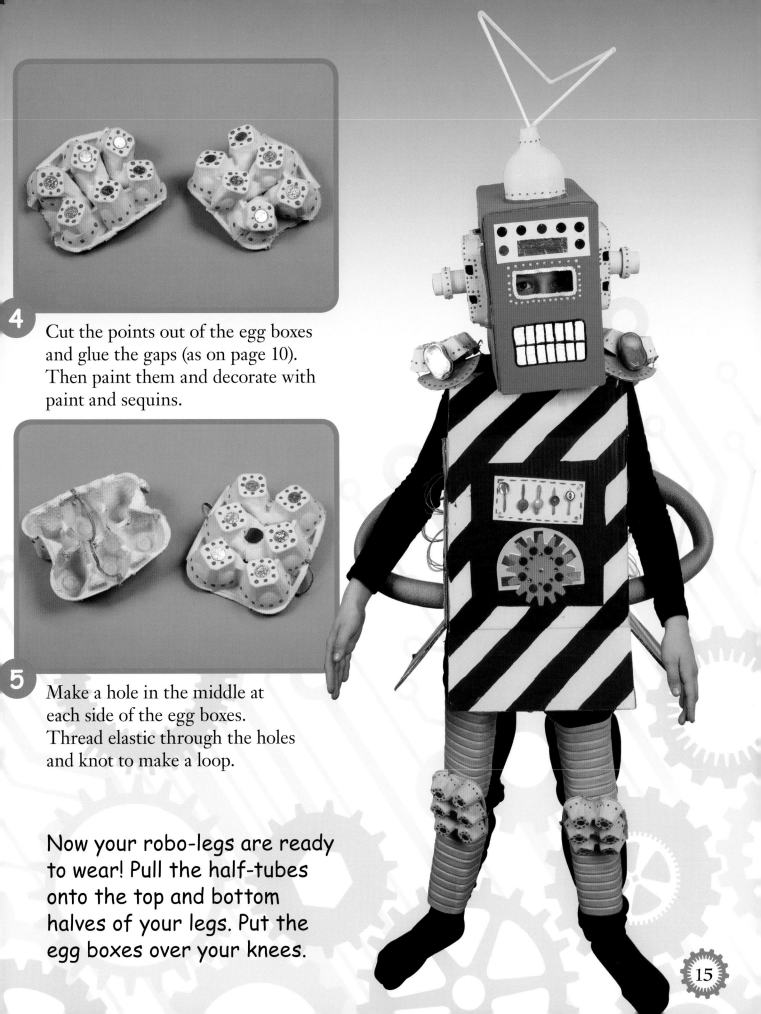

4 Cut the points out of the egg boxes and glue the gaps (as on page 10). Then paint them and decorate with paint and sequins.

5 Make a hole in the middle at each side of the egg boxes. Thread elastic through the holes and knot to make a loop.

Now your robo-legs are ready to wear! Pull the half-tubes onto the top and bottom halves of your legs. Put the egg boxes over your knees.

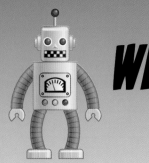

WELL—ARMED

Robots are very good at doing difficult jobs. They need special, **mechanical** arms to help them to do their work.

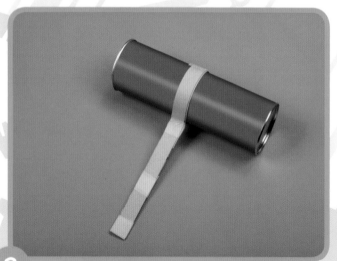

1 Use scissors to cut three strips out of thin cardboard (1 in. by 12 in.).

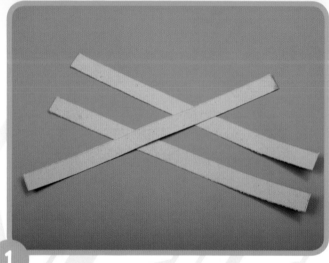

2 Take an empty chip tube and wrap two of the cardboard strips around its middle. Glue them in place.

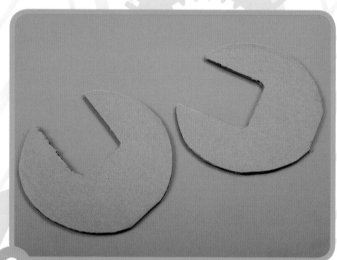

3 Ask an adult to cut two wrench head shapes, 6 in. wide, out of thick cardboard using a craft knife.

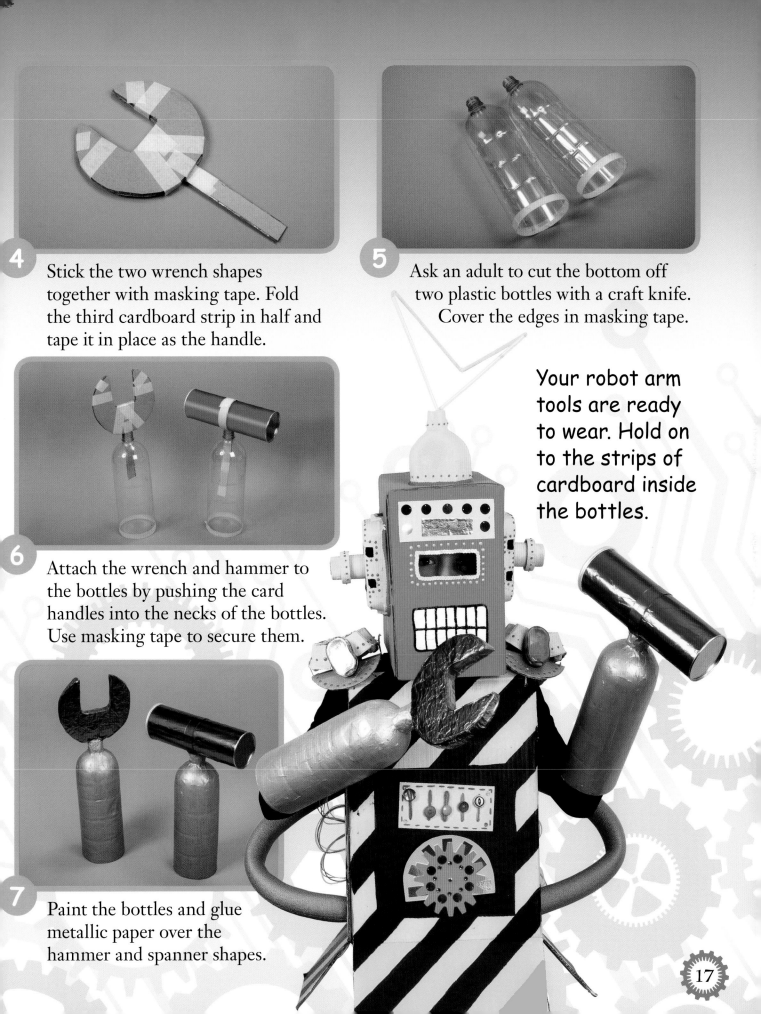

4 Stick the two wrench shapes together with masking tape. Fold the third cardboard strip in half and tape it in place as the handle.

5 Ask an adult to cut the bottom off two plastic bottles with a craft knife. Cover the edges in masking tape.

Your robot arm tools are ready to wear. Hold on to the strips of cardboard inside the bottles.

6 Attach the wrench and hammer to the bottles by pushing the card handles into the necks of the bottles. Use masking tape to secure them.

7 Paint the bottles and glue metallic paper over the hammer and spanner shapes.

BEST FOOT FORWARD

Robots wear big, clumpy shoes and move slowly but steadily in them.

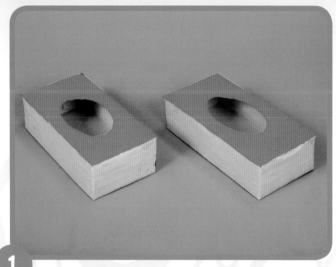

1 Paint the top and sides of two empty tissue boxes.

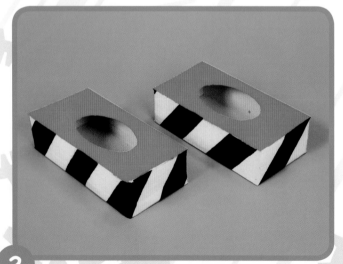

2 Use a ruler to draw stripes around the sides of the boxes and paint stripes in.

3 Add some dots of paint. Make two pairs of small holes either side of the large hole in each box.

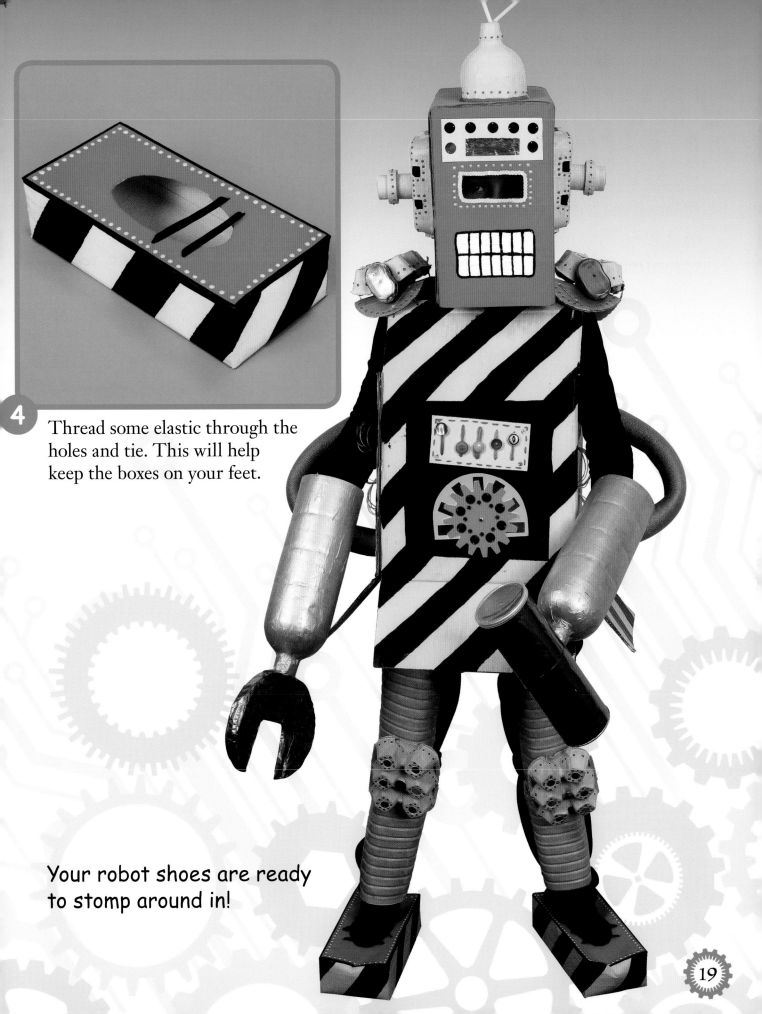

4 Thread some elastic through the holes and tie. This will help keep the boxes on your feet.

Your robot shoes are ready to stomp around in!

THE CUTTING EDGE

A laser tool can cut through metal. This means it is useful for cutting through doors to rescue people.

1 Paint the three small boxes.

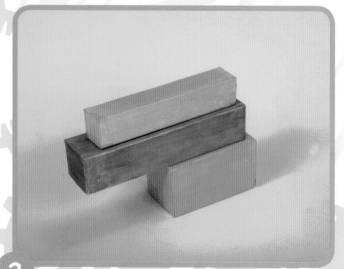

2 Glue the boxes together in a laserlike shape.

3 Glue bottle lids to make buttons on the top of your laser tool.

4 Glue a straw onto a plastic bottle lid. Then glue the lid onto the end of the laser. Decorate the laser with sequins.

Tie the laser to one of your robot arms with elastic. Your laser is ready to use whenever you need to make a quick escape!

A TIN MAN'S BEST FRIEND

A robot's life can be lonely. So why not make a friend?

1 Ask an adult to cut the end off a plastic bottle. Cover the top end of the bottle and a box and juice carton with foil.

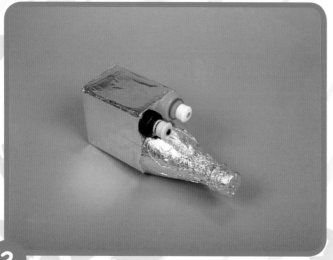

2 Glue the bottle top to the smaller box to make the head and nose. Glue two bottle lids above the nose to make the eyes.

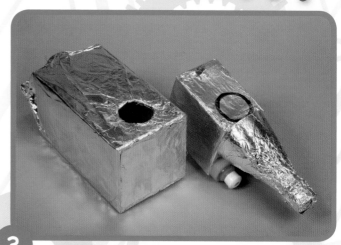

3 Draw around the pipe on the bottom of the head and on the top of the large box. Ask an adult to cut out the circles to make holes.

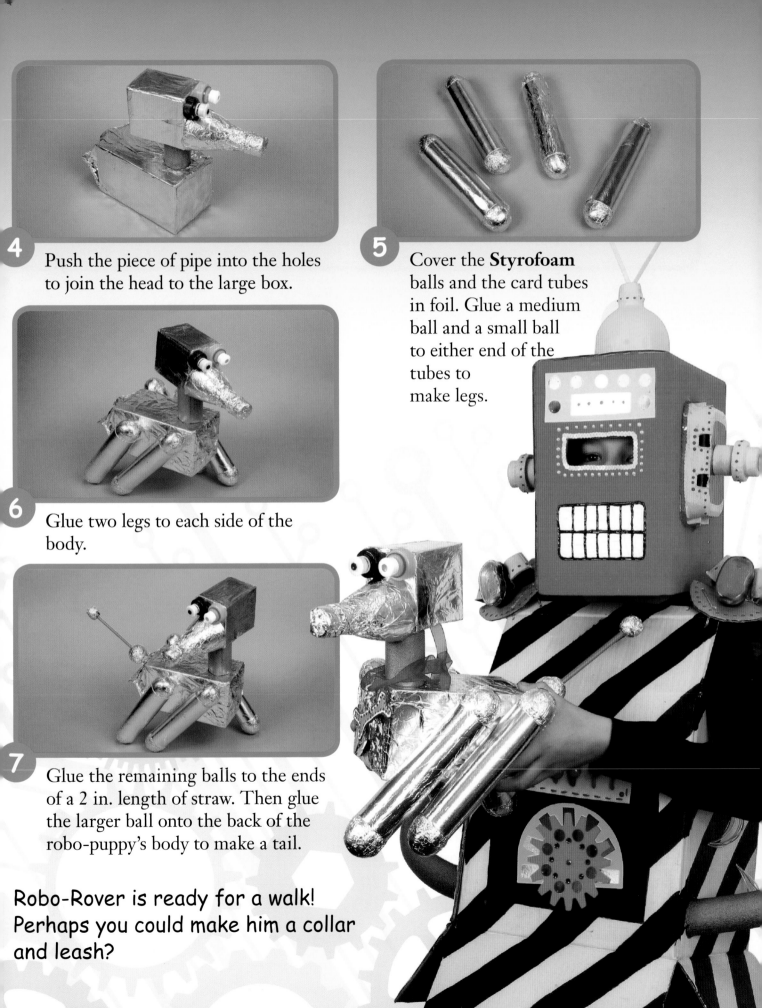

4 Push the piece of pipe into the holes to join the head to the large box.

5 Cover the **Styrofoam** balls and the card tubes in foil. Glue a medium ball and a small ball to either end of the tubes to make legs.

6 Glue two legs to each side of the body.

7 Glue the remaining balls to the ends of a 2 in. length of straw. Then glue the larger ball onto the back of the robo-puppy's body to make a tail.

Robo-Rover is ready for a walk! Perhaps you could make him a collar and leash?

GLOSSARY

antenna (an-TEH-neh) a wire that receives information
attach (uh-TACH) to join one thing to another
lengthwise (LENGKTH-wyz) from one end to the other along the longest side
mechanical (mih-KA-nih-kul) like a machine
snugly (SNUG-lee) close fitting—but not too tight
Styrofoam (STY-ruh-fohm) a white, foamlike material

FURTHER INFORMATION

Bergin, Mark. *Robots (How to Draw).* New York, NY: PowerKids Press, 2008.
Brown, Heather. *The Robot Book.* Riverside, NJ: Andrews McMeel, 2010.
Lucas, David. *The Robot and the Bluebird.* New York, NY: Farrar, Strauss and Giroux, 2008.
Torres, Jickie. *Watch Me Draw Robots.* Minneapolis, MN: Walter Foster Publishing, 2010.

WEB SITES

For Web resources related to the subject of this book, go to:
www.windmillbooks.com/weblinks and select this book's title.

INDEX